Read
And Write

By Lillian Lieberman, James Morrow,
Murray Suid
Illustrated by Corbin Hillam

Publisher: Roberta Suid
Editor: Elizabeth Russell
Cover Design: David Hale
Design and Production: Susan Pinkerton
Cover Art: Corbin Hillam

Monday Morning is a registered trademark
of Monday Morning Books, Inc.

Entire contents copyright © 1986 by Monday Morning
Books, Inc., Box 1680, Palo Alto, California 94302

ISBN 0-912107-54-5

Printed in the United States of America

9 8 7 6 5 4 3 2 1

INTRODUCTION

The *Tab and Lil* reading books are high-interest preprimers and primers based on sight vocabulary words. The picture-story theme relates the adventures of Tab and Lil, who play host to Og, a whimsical being from outer space.

Each book contains six stories accompanied by worksheets. The worksheets in each book emphasize different skills and concepts needed in learning to read. Some stories are open-ended for the child to complete creatively by drawing or writing original dialogue.

BOOK I: READY TO READ emphasizes readiness skills and concepts including directional orientation, size, colors, shapes, closure, visual discrimination, consonants, rhyming, and sequencing.

BOOK II: START TO READ emphasizes reading skills. Activities include word discrimination and recognition, phrase and sentence reading and comprehension, rhyming, cause and effect and simple inference skills, following directions, story sequencing, reading mini-stories, and answering simple questions.

BOOK III: READ AND WRITE emphasizes reading and writing skills, including copying and writing words and simple phrases, and writing original dialogue for stories.

Other skills practiced in worksheet activities are cutting and pasting, matching, coloring, drawing, circling, and copying.

Sight words are repeated throughout the three readers and in the worksheets. Phonetic words are added to balance the program. Content words help to carry out the story line. The picture sequences aid in associating meaning with the words and give clues to the words themselves.

The imaginative content of the readers motivates and stimulates the beginning reader to learn the basic words necessary for success in more formal reading instruction. Special Education and English as a Second Language classes may benefit from using these books.

An alphabetical listing of the words used in the books is included for student reference. This list was compiled from the Dolch List, a list of 220 high-frequency prereading sight vocabulary words.

General Directions

INTRODUCE the *Tab and Lil* books by presenting the words necessary before each story sequence. Write the words on the chalkboard or on large cards. Discuss elements of the words to help children learn them, for example, consonants, vowels, rhyming endings, and configuration. Have the children use the words and phrases meaningfully in oral sentences, games, or directions. Make short teacher-class cooperative story charts with the vocabulary words that the children can refer to. Have the children make and illustrate their own stories to share with the class or parents.

MOTIVATE the reading of the stories by telling the children that they are going to meet three characters who have some interesting adventures. Their many adventures are told in picture sequences and simple sentences. Aid the reading and discussion by asking questions such as:

— What are the characters doing? Who are they? What are they like?
— What are they saying? Why? Where do they live? How do they feel?
— What is happening? Why is it happening? What will happen next?
— What other details do you notice? How would you change or end the stories?
— What do you think might happen in the next episode?

3

EXTEND the readers with the worksheets to give more practice and reinforcement for sight vocabulary, simple phonics and phonetic analysis, simple concept development, comprehension, and writing skills.

ENCOURAGE and help the children to read and follow the directions on each page. The simple exercises are designed to give added support to learn words presented in the stories and to practice other readiness and reading skills.

Encourage children to use the story content and words to aid them in drawing conclusions and in writing their own endings.

ENJOY creative play using these different adventures of Tab, Lil, and Og. Children can draw or make up their own funny incidents and act them out. Such activities will create on-going motivation and interest for the adventures of Tab, Lil, and Og.

After completing the stories, children can take them home to share and practice their new skills.

"Read and Write" Skills List

Readiness Skills:

Concept recognition and discrimination:
  colors: brown, orange
  numbers: one - ten
  directions: in, out, up, down, before, after
Sequencing:
  picture sequences
  letter sequence in words
  word sequence in phrases and sentences
Closure:
  words to be traced
Visual discrimination:
  pictures, details
  words
Sight word reinforcement
Fine motor skills:
  tracing, copying, circling
  cutting, pasting, coloring
  drawing

Word Identification Skills:

Clues:
  pictures

word forms
  meaning
  letters
Phonetic analysis:
  rhyme elements
  sound-symbol association

Comprehension Skills:

Literal meaning:
  naming objects and characters in pictures
  identifying details
  following directions
  answering simple questions
Interpreting:
  interpreting pictures and picture sequences
  categorizing
  anticipating and predicting outcomes
  sequencing, cause and effect, before and after
  drawing conclusions
  making inferences using picture clues
  word-picture associations (relationships)
  interpreting word, phrase, sentence meaning
  writing words in context

WORD LIST

a	get	me	soon
am	go	Miss	stay
and	good	miss	
are	Grandma	Mom	Tab
	Grandpa	my	talk
			ten
back		night	thank
ball	have	nine	that
be	help	no	the
Bill	here		this
buy	hide		three
	hill	Og	time
can	home	Og's	to
cold	hot	on	too
come	how	one	town
	hunt	orange	trip
day		our	try
do	I	out	T V
dog	is		
don't	it	park	two
down		play	
drink	Jim	please	up
	jump		
eat		read	walk
eight	know		want
		school	way
find	let's	seek	we
five	like	ship	what
food	Lil	shop	will
for	look	show	write
found		sit	
four		six	you
fun		some	your
funny			

Puppet Patterns

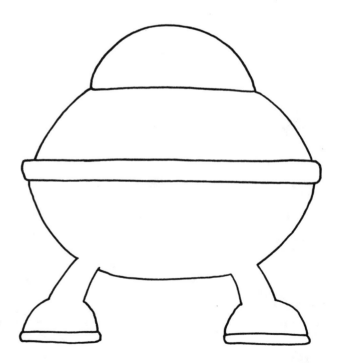

6

The Shop

Name_____

One or two? Write the word. Color.

one   two

_____

_____

_____

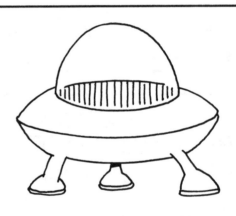

_____

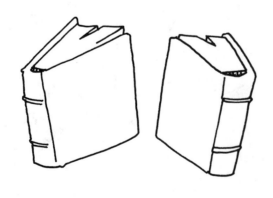

_____

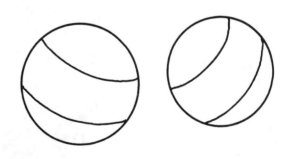

_____

Cut and paste in order.

1	2	3

Stop and shop. Cut and paste words that rhyme with shop.

hop	cap	top	pen
pig	mop	wet	pop

Draw the picture. Color.

my   my   my

my hand	my home
my pet	my hat

Draw something in the shop.

OPEN

Name_____

Read. Write the word. Color.

Here is a _____.

Come buy some_____.

Here is_____.

We are _____TV.

Take_____home, Og.

on shop us Og food

Skill: literal meaning

Read	Trace	Write
one	one	
us	us	
buy	buy	

(Ring) the words that are the same.

one	on one no one
us	is us us as
buy	buy boy buy bat

Hide and Seek

18

Name_____

Draw the number of things.

three   four   five   six

3   4   5   6

six hats	three bats
five balls	four cans

Name_____

Color the 🎃 if the words are the same.

🎃	and and
🎃	be he
🎃	don't don't
🎃	is is
🎃	find mind
🎃	stay stay
🎃	here here

Name_____

Cut and paste the words that match the pictures.

and   and   and

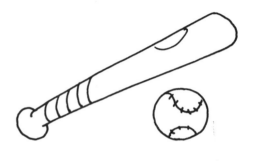

cat and dog

Tab and Lil

Mom and Dad

bat and ball

Name_____

Color the bones that rhyme with dog.

log

fog

top

hot

frog

go

hog

bog

Skill: phonetic analysis

© 1986 Monday Morning Books, Inc.

Cut and paste what is <u>in</u> or <u>out</u>. Color.

in　　　　　　　　out

Name

Cut and paste. Match the words to the pictures. Color.

hide   play   back   dog

hide and seek	sack on my back
dog on a log	stay and play

Name_____

Read	Trace	Write
out	out	- - - - -
walk	walk	- - - - -
find	find	- - - - -

(Ring) the words that are the same.

out	out two our out
walk	talk walk wall walk
find	find mind find fin

Skill: sight word reinforcement   © 1986 Monday Morning Books, Inc.

Halloween Trip

28

29

Color the things you can take on a trip.

trip

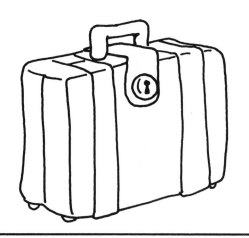

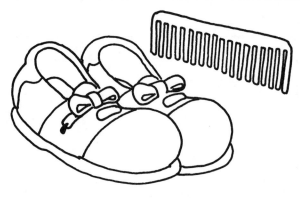

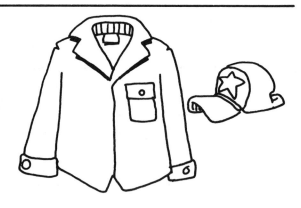

Name_____

Cut and paste. Match the sentence with the picture.

I like to <u>bake</u>.

I sit by the <u>lake</u>.

This is a <u>cake</u>.

I like to <u>rake</u>.

(Ring) the words that are the same.

will	will it will him
soon	moon soon soon on
back	back sack walk back
school	school pool school tool
know	how know draw know
trip	up trip trip it

Name_____

Cut and paste. Match the sentences.

have   have   have

I have to read.

I have to go up.

I have to go out.

I have to play.

Skill: literal meaning

© 1986 Monday Morning Books, Inc.

Name_____

Write the word.

be   hill   come   want   here

I will_____back soon.

Bill can run up the_____.

Can you_____and play?

I_____to read.

Come_____!

Name _____

Write the words that match the picture.

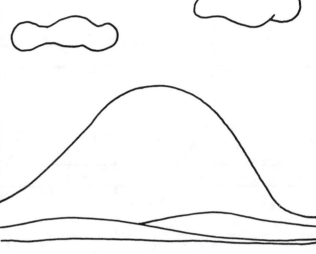

This is _____.

a lake   a school

This is_____.

a school   a hill

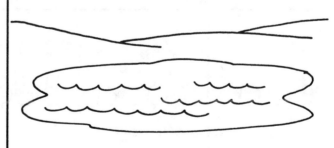

Here is_____.

Tab   Grandma

This is _____.

a hill   a lake

Name_____

Read	Trace	Write
soon	soon	- - - - - -
read	read	- - - - - -
want	want	- - - - - -

(Ring) the words that are the same.

soon	noon soon moon soon
read	road dear read read
want	won't want went want

School

39

Match the word with the picture.
Draw a line.

seven	eight	nine	ten
7	8	9	10

ten

nine

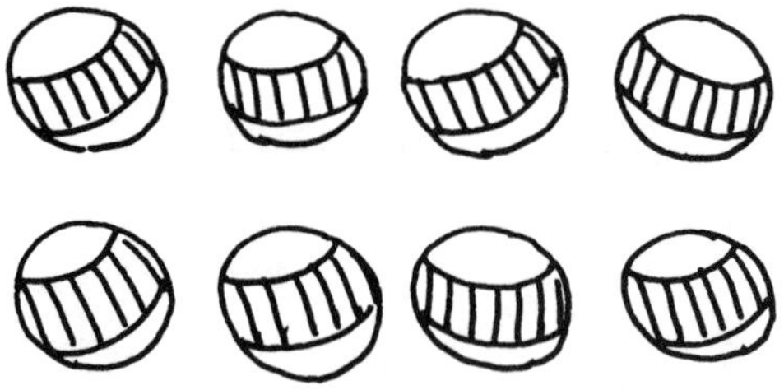

eight

seven

Name_____

Write the word.

eat   play   read   school

I like to _____.

I like to _____.

I like to _____.

I like _____.

Name_____

Cut and paste the sentence that matches the picture.

This is our school!

Come and read.

This is my ship.

Five + five are ten.

Name_____

Write the words in a sentence.

my school is This

_____

_____

_____

and read Come

_____

_____

_____

with is Lil Tab

_____

_____

my This is ship

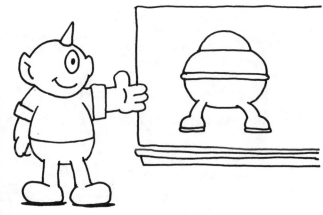

_____

_____

Name

Color ◁[orange] words that rhyme with way.

way

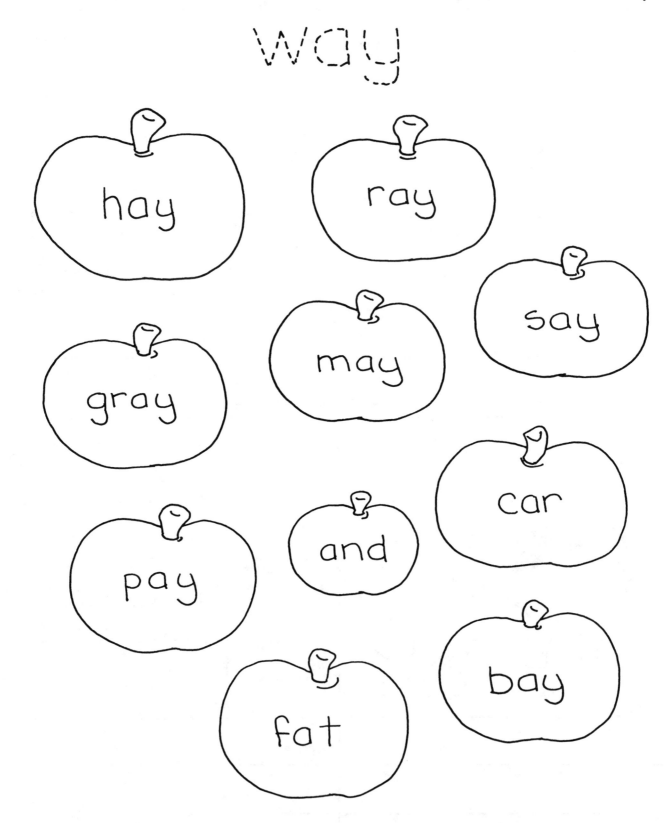

hay

ray

gray

may

say

pay

and

car

fat

bay

Skill: phonetic analysis

© 1986 Monday Morning Books, Inc.

Name_____

Read	Trace	Write
eat	eat	
our	our	
two	two	

Write the word.

eat   our   two

I like to _____ food.

One and one = _____.

$1 + 1 = 2$

This is ____ school.

The Park

You write it.

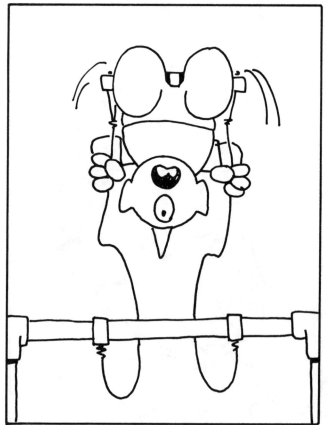

You end it.

Ring the word.

Og can go up and ___.
town   down   brown

Lil can go in and ___.
our   on   out

Tab can ___ in the park.
say   play   may

It is ___ to play.
bun   run   fun

Up and Down

Og is in the park.
Og can go up.
Og can go down.
Og can go up and down in the park.

1. Who can go up? _____

2. Who can go down? _____

3. What can Og do? _____

_____

4. Can Og go up and down?
yes or no [ ]

Cut and paste what comes next.

1	2

1	2

1	2

Name_____

Ring the sentence that matches the picture.

Og is in the ship.

Tab is in the ship.

Here is the city.

Here is the park.

Lil can go up and down.

Og can go in and out.

Tab can go up.

Tab can go out.

Name_____

In and Out

Cut on the ┊ line.

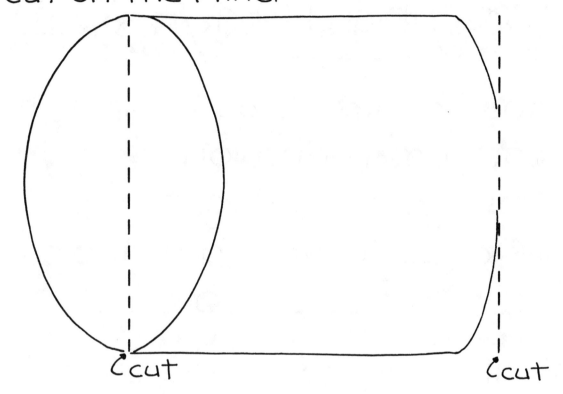

ᒐcut   ᒐcut

Cut. Make Og, Lil, and Tab go in and out.

Lil and Tab like to go in and out.
Lil can go in and out.
Tab can go in and out.
Can Og go in and out, too?
Yes _____ No _____

1. Who likes to go in and out?
_____ and _____
2. Where can Tab and Lil go?
_____ and _____
3. Who can go in and out, too?
_____
4. Can you go in and out, too?
Yes or No [____]

Name_____

Cut and paste. <u>Where</u> is Og?

at home

at the park

at school

in the shop

Good-bye

You write it!

Draw Og's home.

Name_____

Time to Go

Og is in the ship.
The ship is up.
It is time for Og to go.
Good-bye, Og!

1. Who is in the ship?

_____

2. Where is the ship?

_____

3. What must Og do?

_____

4. What do we say to Og?

_____

Good Food

The food is good.
It is not too hot.
It is not too cold.
The food is good to eat.

1. What is good?

_____

2. Is the food too hot? Make an X.

Yes ☐   No ☐

3. Is the food too cold? Make an X.

Yes ☐   No ☐

4. What is the food good for?

_____

Name_____

Is it hot or cold? Cut and paste.

hot	cold

Name_____

Is it night or day? Cut and paste.

night	day

Write the word. Color.

good   hot   cold   night

This is_____.

This is_____.

This is_____.

These are_____.

Name_____

Read	Trace	Write
had	had	
good	good	
cold	cold	

(Ring) the words that are the same.

had	had hid dad had
good	cook good hood good
cold	cold gold cold come